THIS WALKER BOOK BELONGS TO:

_____

_____

_____

First published 2022 by Walker Books Ltd, 87 Vauxhall Walk, London SE11 5HJ
in association with Historic Royal Palaces, Hampton Court Palace, Surrey KT8 9AU

Some content originally published 2016 as *Pop-Up Kings and Queens*

2 4 6 8 10 9 7 5 3 1

© 2016, 2022 Walker Books Ltd

Illustrations by Rachael Saunders

This book has been typeset in Voltaire and Active

Printed in Lithuania

All rights reserved. No part of this book may be reproduced, transmitted or stored in an information retrieval system in any form or by any means, graphic, electronic or mechanical, including photocopying, taping and recording, without prior written permission from the publisher.

British Library Cataloguing in Publication Data: a catalogue record for this book is available from the British Library

ISBN 978-1-5295-1320-2

www.walker.co.uk

WALKER BOOKS
AND SUBSIDIARIES
LONDON · BOSTON · SYDNEY · AUCKLAND

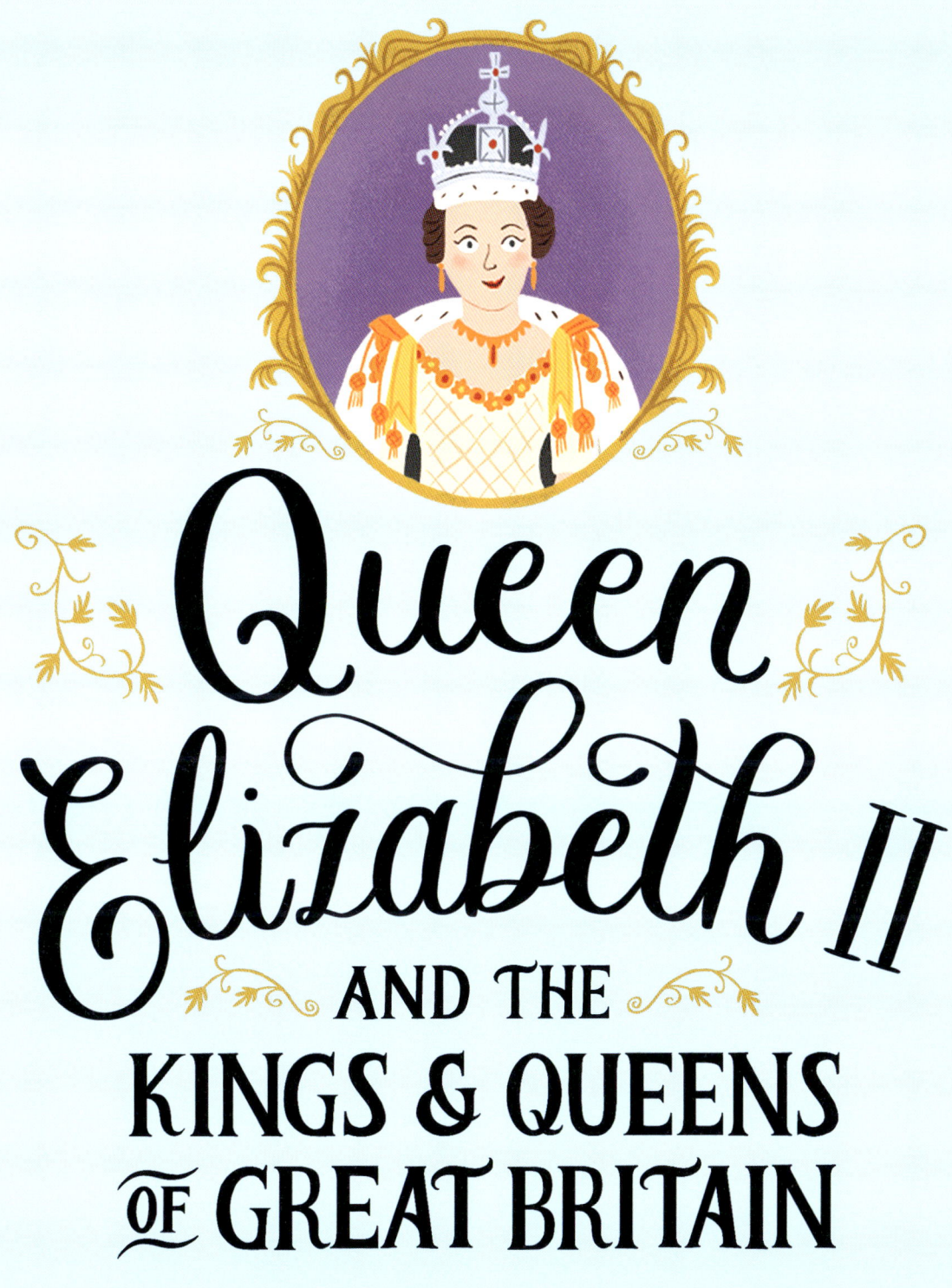

Queen Elizabeth II
AND THE KINGS & QUEENS OF GREAT BRITAIN

ILLUSTRATED BY RACHAEL SAUNDERS

QUEEN ELIZABETH II

In 2022, when she was 96 years old, Queen Elizabeth II celebrated her Platinum Jubilee, which commemorated an astonishing 70 years on the throne. The next-longest-reigning British monarch was Elizabeth's great-great-grandmother, Queen Victoria, who reigned for 63 years.

A Future Queen

Elizabeth Alexandra Mary was born on 21 April 1926, to Prince Albert and Princess Elizabeth, the Duke and Duchess of York. Elizabeth's childhood nickname was "Lilibet" as she couldn't pronounce "Elizabeth". Her father would later become King George VI, making Elizabeth the heir to throne.

Palace Pets

As a child, Elizabeth's favourite animals were dogs and horses – passions that she maintained all her life. Elizabeth and her younger sister, Princess Margaret, were given their first corgi in 1933 by their father. They named him Dookie.

Second World War

Elizabeth was only thirteen at the start of World War Two. She and Margaret were sent to Windsor Castle to avoid the bombing raids, while her parents remained at Buckingham Palace. In 1944, when Elizabeth turned eighteen, she joined the Auxiliary Territorial Service (ATS), the women's branch of the British Army. Princess Elizabeth began her training in March 1945 and was nicknamed "Princess Auto Mechanic".

The Royal Wedding

Elizabeth's wedding to Philip Mountbatten took place on 20 November 1947 at Westminster Abbey. On that day, Prince Philip became Duke of Edinburgh, Earl of Merioneth and Baron Greenwich. Elizabeth had eight bridesmaids, including her sister Margaret, and 2,000 guests. The couple received over 2,500 wedding presents from around the world. During their marriage, Elizabeth and Philip had four children: Prince Charles, Princess Anne, Prince Andrew and Prince Edward. Sadly, after over 70 years of marriage, Philip died in 2021 at the age of 99.

The Crown Jewels

The Crown Jewels are still worn by members of the Royal Family today. At the heart of the collection is the Coronation Regalia used since 1661 to crown the kings and queens of England.

The Coronation

Elizabeth's Coronation took place on 2 June 1953 at Westminster Abbey, where coronations have been held for 900 years. During the ceremony Elizabeth took the Coronation Oath and was anointed with holy oil before being crowned with St Edward's Crown by the Archbishop of Canterbury.

Elizabeth arrived at the Coronation in the Gold State Coach – pulled by eight grey horses: Cunningham, Tovey, Noah, Tedder, Eisenhower, Snow White, Tipperary and McCreery.

Must-Watch TV

Elizabeth's Coronation was the first to be shown on television, which was quite a new invention at the time. Over 20 million people tuned in from the UK alone and millions more around the world.

The Commonwealth

The Commonwealth is a group of diverse and independent nations from all over the world which are historically linked to Britain. As Head of the Commonwealth, Elizabeth's reign commenced with her longest-ever Commonwealth tour, lasting from November 1953 to May 1954. She was the first reigning British monarch to visit Australia and New Zealand, and she became the most widely travelled monarch in history.

Jubilee Celebrations

There have been celebratory milestones throughout Elizabeth's reign. Elizabeth celebrated her Silver Jubilee in 1977, her Golden Jubilee in 2002 and her Diamond Jubilee in 2012. At her Platinum Jubilee, she opened the Elizabeth line in London. Many people all over Britain and the rest of the world joined in with the celebrations by holding street parties.

THE NORMANS
1066-1154

The monarchy, as we know it today, was founded over 1,000 years before the reign of Elizabeth II. In 1066, King Edward the Confessor died without any children. He named his brother-in-law Harold as heir to the English throne – but then a French duke named William of Normandy said he had been promised the crown. William invaded England and defeated Harold at the Battle of Hastings. He became known as "William the Conqueror", and he was the first Norman King of England.

William I (1066-1087)

William the Conqueror was crowned on Christmas Day 1066, but he soon returned to France and spent hardly any of his reign in England. English nobles hated him because he took their land and titles away and gave them to French aristocrats.

Royal Castles

William the Conqueror built 80 castles to defend his new kingdom from attack. The most famous is the White Tower, now part of the Tower of London.

1066

WILLIAM I
1066-1087

The Tower of London

When the White Tower was built, it was one of the biggest fortresses in England. Over the years, kings and queens added to the site, and the Tower of London became a prison, a place of execution, even a zoo – wild animals were kept there from 1210 to 1832. Now the Tower is home to the Crown Jewels and is one of the world's most popular tourist attractions.

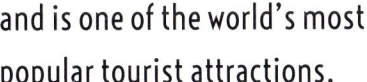

The Domesday Book

William ordered a survey to find out how much land and property everyone in England owned. The information was written up in the Domesday Book. The original copy still exists today, over 900 years after it was written.

Feudal System

When William became king, he governed England the Norman way. Instead of paying with money, people paid with services. This was called the feudal system. At the top, barons were given land for providing knights to the king. Peasants were at the bottom and grew crops in return for protection.

The Bayeux Tapestry

The story of William I's invasion is told in the Bayeux Tapestry, an amazing 70-metre long embroidery made in around 1070.

William II (1087-1100)

King William II was known as "Rufus", which means red, because he had bright red cheeks. He had a fiery temper, too – he fought with the church, the King of Scotland, and both his brothers. William was killed by an arrow while he was hunting. Some people think his brother Henry had him killed so that he could become king.

Angry Archbishop

William II had a very difficult relationship with the church and he was openly critical of religion, which was very unusual at the time. William angered the church by selling church offices (bishoprics) or keeping them empty so he could take the money for himself. William finally appointed Anselm of Bec as the Archbishop of Canterbury in 1093. However, the two strongly disagreed with each other and William seized Anslem's property.

WILLIAM II
1087-1100

HENRY I
1100-1135

Henry I (1100-1135)

King Henry I only had two children with his wife – William and Matilda – but at least twenty with his many mistresses. In 1120, William drowned when the boat he was sailing in, the *White Ship*, sank, so Henry made Matilda his heir. Legend says Henry died of food poisoning after eating too many lampreys (eel-like fish).

Stephen (1135-1154)

King Stephen stole the crown from his cousin, Matilda. The English nobles supported him because they didn't think a woman could rule, but Matilda didn't give up. She and Stephen fought a civil war known as The Anarchy for twenty years.

Matilda

Matilda almost became queen in 1141. She defeated Stephen in battle, and went to Westminster Abbey to be crowned, but when she arrived she was so rude that the crowds turned on her and she had to run away. Eventually Stephen and Matilda agreed that Stephen could keep the crown but Matilda's son Henry would become king when Stephen died. So you could say Matilda won in the end.

THE PLANTAGENETS
1154-1485

After the death of Stephen, the last Norman king, his nephew became Henry II, the first Plantagenet king. The Plantagenets were great warriors. They fought France in the Hundred Years' War, led the bloody Crusades – and they even fought each other! The Plantagenet dynasty ended when two branches of the family turned on each other in a civil war – the Wars of the Roses.

John (1199-1216)

King John is famous as the villain in the Robin Hood legends. He raised unfair taxes to pay for wars with France, and eventually his barons rebelled against him. In June 1215, they forced him to sign the Magna Carta, a peace treaty which said that monarchs had to obey the law and guaranteed "free men" the right to a fair trial.

1154

HENRY II
1154-1189

RICHARD I
1189-1199

JOHN
1199-1216

Richard II (1377-1399)

Richard II was just ten when he became king. He wasn't popular – he spent huge amounts of money and he didn't think kings should have to listen to advice. In 1399, Richard was overthrown by his cousin, Henry. He was imprisoned in Pontefract Castle, where he starved to death.

The Peasants' Revolt

In 1381, a group of working people rebelled when the government tried to collect taxes from them. They travelled to London, stormed the Tower of London and demanded an end to unfair taxes and forced labour. Thirteen-year-old Richard II met the rebels and agreed to their demands, but many were later rounded up and executed.

The Canterbury Tales

Geoffrey Chaucer worked for Richard II as a diplomat. In his spare time, he wrote some of the greatest works of English literature, including *The Canterbury Tales*, a collection of stories about a group of pilgrims on their way to Canterbury Cathedral.

HENRY III	EDWARD I	EDWARD II	EDWARD III	RICHARD II
1216-1272	1272-1307	1307-1327	1327-1377	1377-1399

Henry V (1413-1422)

Henry V spent most of his short reign trying to become King of France. He almost managed it – he beat the French at the Battle of Agincourt in 1415, but he died before he could take the throne.

Richard III (1483-1485)

Richard III is regarded as one of England's most unpopular kings, partly because Shakespeare wrote a play portraying him as a ruthless murderer. He was the last English king to die in battle, and in 2012 his long-lost remains were discovered beneath a car park.

The Princes in the Tower

Richard III stole the crown from his nephew, Edward V. He had Edward and his brother Richard imprisoned in the Tower of London. When Edward V and his brother were locked up in the Tower of London, they became known as the Princes in the Tower. After Richard III was crowned in 1483, they were never seen again. Most people think Richard had them murdered.

HENRY IV
1399-1413

HENRY V
1413-1422

HENRY VI
1422-1461

The Wars of the Roses

For 30 years, a civil war raged between two branches of the Plantagenet family: the House of York and the House of Lancaster. The Yorkists' symbol was a white rose, and the Lancastrians' was a red rose, so the conflict was named the Wars of the Roses.

The Battle of Bosworth

In 1485, the deciding battle of the Wars of the Roses took place between Richard III and Henry Tudor. During the battle, Richard's chief commanders swapped sides and the enraged king died before he could have his revenge.

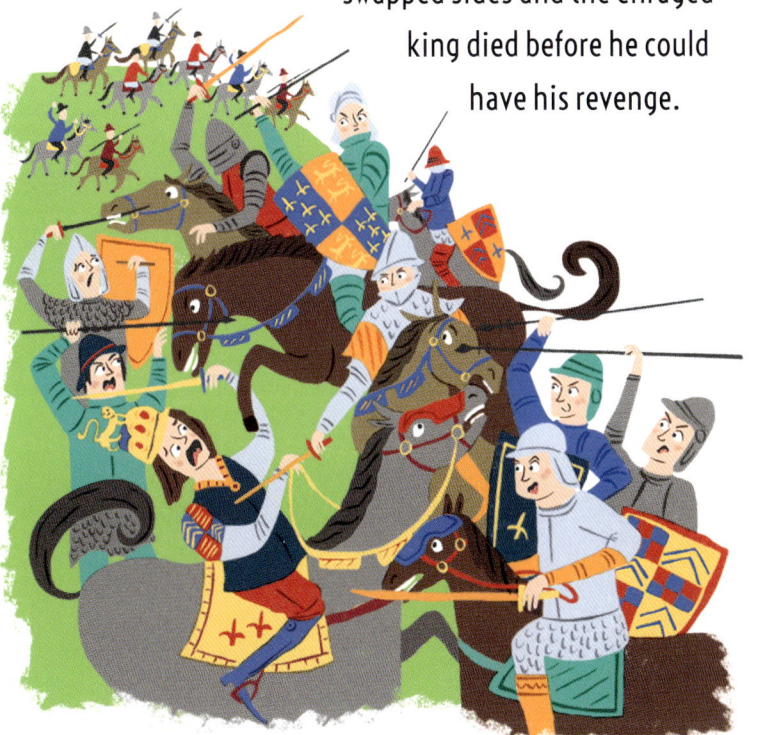

The End of the Plantagenets

The Wars of the Roses ended when a Lancastrian named Henry Tudor killed Yorkist Richard III at the Battle of Bosworth. Henry married Elizabeth of York to unite the two sides. He created a new symbol, the Tudor Rose, by joining the red rose of Lancaster with the white rose of York.

RED ROSE OF LANCASTER

WHITE ROSE OF YORK

TUDOR ROSE

1485

EDWARD IV
1461-1483

EDWARD V
1483

RICHARD III
1483-1485

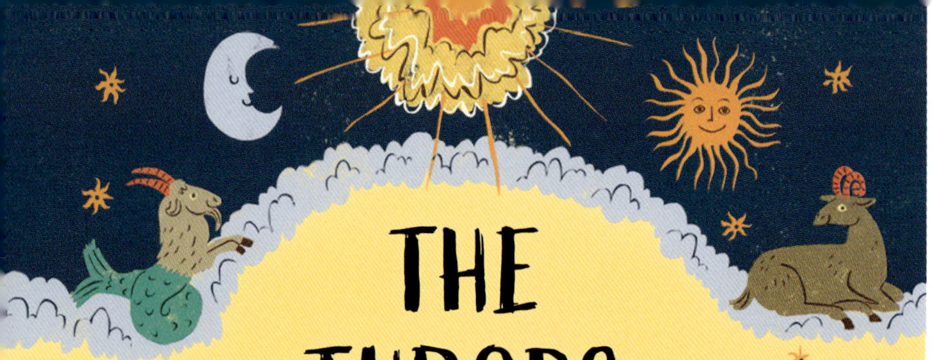

THE TUDORS
1485-1603

The Tudors are probably the most famous monarchs of all time. During the 118 years that they reigned, the Church of England was established, Shakespeare wrote some of his best plays and the first female monarchs of England, Mary and Elizabeth I, proved women could rule just as well as men.

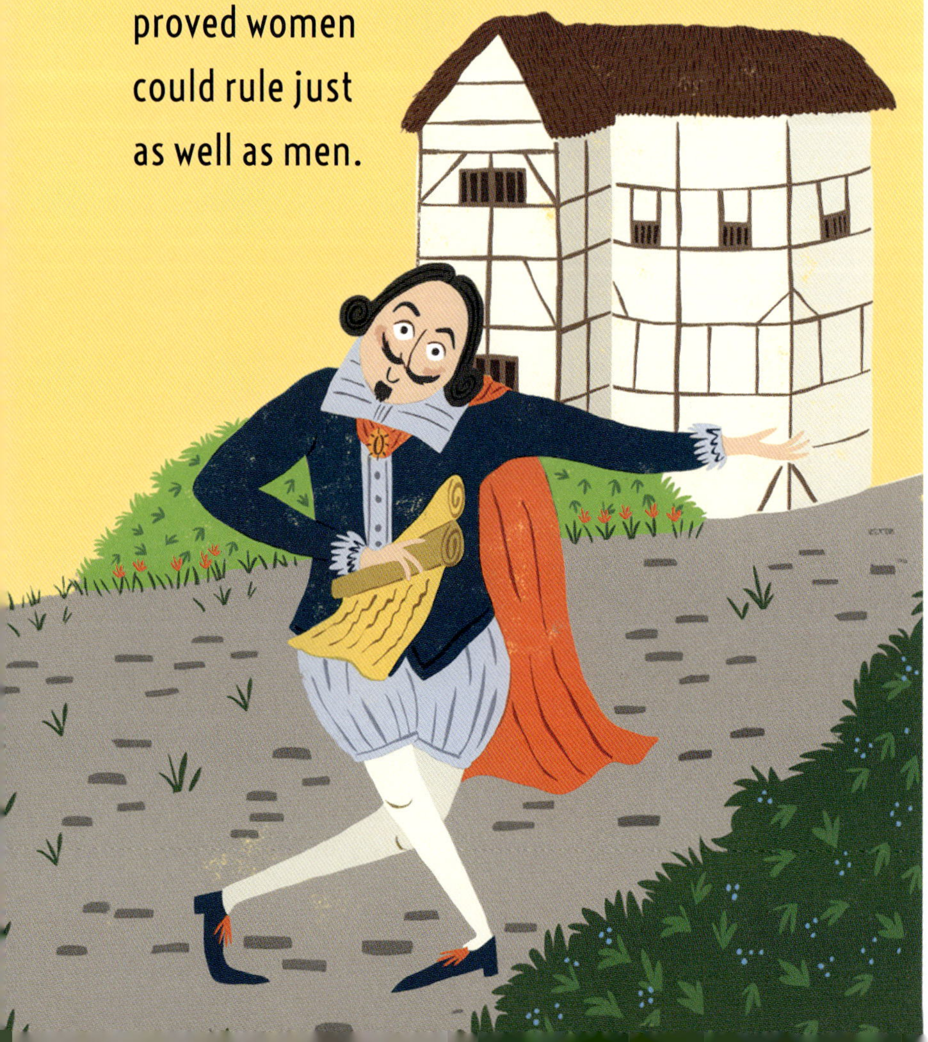

Henry VIII (1509-1547)

As a young man, Henry VIII was charming and sporty, but as he grew older, he became fat and bad-tempered. Henry was desperate for a son, but his first wife, Katherine of Aragon, only had a girl. He asked the Pope if he could divorce her, but the Pope said no. So Henry left the Catholic Church and gave himself a divorce.

1485

HENRY VII
1485-1509

Hampton Court

Henry VIII's favourite palace was Hampton Court. It had tennis courts, huge kitchens and a lavatory known as the Great House of Easement that could seat fourteen people at a time. You can still visit the palace today.

HENRY VIII
1509-1547

The Church of England

Henry made himself the head of his own church, the Church of England, and destroyed the Catholic monasteries, seizing Church land for himself. The British monarch is still Head of the Church of England today.

After Henry divorced Katherine of Aragon, he married one of her ladies-in-waiting, Anne Boleyn. He hoped Anne would give birth to a son, but she had a daughter, too. Henry had her executed. He married four more times; his third wife, Jane Seymour, had a boy, but died soon afterwards. Henry was buried next to Jane when he died.

Henry VIII's Wives

King Henry VIII is famous for marrying six times. Marrying Henry was a dangerous business – he had two of his wives executed.

DIVORCED
Katherine of Aragon
Queen 1509-1533

BEHEADED
Anne Boleyn
Queen 1533-1536

DIED
Jane Seymour
Queen 1536-1537

DIVORCED
Anne of Cleves
Queen 1540

BEHEADED
Catherine Howard
Queen 1540-1542

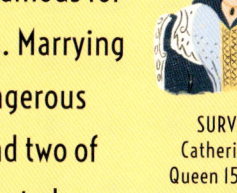
SURVIVED!
Catherine Parr
Queen 1543-1547

Edward VI (1547-1553)

King Edward VI was Henry VIII's longed-for son. He became king aged nine, so England was governed by his advisors. He was a Protestant, and he didn't want his Catholic sister Mary to inherit the throne, so he named Lady Jane Grey, daughter-in-law of his chief advisor, as his heir.

Mary I (1553-1558)

Lady Jane Grey was queen for just nine days before she was overthrown by Henry VIII's eldest daughter Mary. Mary tried to make England Catholic again. She earned the nickname "Bloody Mary" because she had over 300 people burned at the stake for refusing to become Catholic.

Elizabeth I (1558-1603)

Queen Elizabeth I had to fend off several people who wanted her crown, including her own cousin, Mary Queen of Scots, and her sister's husband, Philip II of Spain. Philip proposed to Elizabeth after Mary died. Elizabeth refused. Elizabeth didn't want to share her power with anyone, so she stayed single and said she was married to her country. She was known as the "Virgin Queen".

Elizabeth's wardrobe was full of gowns made from rich fabrics adorned with jewels and elaborate detail.

EDWARD VI
1547-1553

English Explorers

The most famous explorers were Sir Francis Drake and Sir Walter Raleigh. Sir Francis was a brilliant sailor, sailing round the world between 1577-1580, and eventually helping Elizabeth to defeat the Spanish Armada. In 1584, Sir Walter sailed to North America in search of treasure.

The Spanish Armada

In 1588, Philip attempted to invade England, sending 130 Spanish ships. The Armada was hit by strong storms and defeated by Elizabeth's highly skilled commanders.

Royal Favourites

Although she never married, Elizabeth did have "favourites" – men she spent time with and showered with gifts. Elizabeth was very jealous and didn't want her favourites to marry. When she found out that Sir Walter had secretly married one of her ladies-in-waiting, she had them both locked up in the Tower of London.

William Shakespeare

Elizabeth loved the theatre. The most popular playwright of the time was William Shakespeare, who wrote a flattering speech about her in *A Midsummer Night's Dream*.

MARY I
1553-1558

ELIZABETH I
1558-1603

THE STUARTS
1603-1649, 1660-1714

Queen Elizabeth I died without children, so she named her cousin, James VI of Scotland, as her heir. He became James I, the first Stuart King of England, and the first monarch to rule England, Scotland and Ireland. The Stuarts reigned for 111 troublesome years. During that time, the Great Plague hit Britain, the Great Fire of London destroyed the capital, and James's son, Charles I, lost his head in the Civil War.

James I (1603-1625)

King James I was a religious man who ordered a new translation of the Bible and opposed witchcraft. He was terrified of being assassinated, and wore padded clothes to protect himself. It turned out he was right to be scared — in 1605, a group of Catholic terrorists planned to blow up Parliament while he was there. The plot to kill James I was known as the Gunpowder Plot. A letter warned Parliament just in time, and one of the plotters, Guy Fawkes, was caught with barrels of gunpowder. Every year, people celebrate the discovery of the plot on 5 November with bonfires and fireworks.

Witchcraft

During James I's reign, many people, mainly women, were tortured and killed for being "witches". James even wrote a book about witchcraft, *Daemonologie*, which inspired parts of Shakespeare's *Macbeth*.

Charles I (1625-1649)

King Charles I didn't think he should have to listen to Members of Parliament, and he ruled without them for eleven years. In 1642, civil war broke out between Charles and Parliament. Parliament won, and Charles was executed for treason. Charles was beheaded at the Banqueting House in London on 30 January 1649. He asked for an extra shirt so he wouldn't shiver from the cold – he didn't want the crowd to think he was afraid.

1603

1649

JAMES I
1603-1625

CHARLES I
1625-1649

Oliver Cromwell and the Civil War

After the Civil War, England was ruled by Oliver Cromwell, who oversaw a government known as the Commonwealth for eleven years. Oliver Cromwell was a Member of Parliament who led Parliament to victory in the Civil War and governed the country as "Lord Protector" after Charles I's death. He was very religious and believed people should lead simple lives. He banned swearing, drinking, plays, Christmas and Easter celebrations, and going for a walk on a Sunday.

Charles II (1660-1685)

Charles II went into exile when his father, Charles I, lost the Civil War. But when Oliver Cromwell died, Charles was invited to become king. He was known as the "Merry Monarch" and had many mistresses, but early in his reign he had to deal with two tragic events: the Great Plague and the Great Fire of London.

1660

CHARLES II
1660-1685

The Great Plague

In 1665, a deadly plague swept through Britain, killing around 100,000 people. Symptoms included swellings in the neck, and most people died within a week of being infected. Red crosses painted on plague victims' doors warned people to stay away.

The Great Fire of London

At 1 a.m. on Sunday 2 September 1666, a fire broke out in a bakery in Pudding Lane, London, and spread across the city. Charles II ordered houses to be pulled down to stop it spreading, and even helped fight the fire himself, but the flames destroyed a third of the city and left 100,000 people homeless.

William and Mary
(Mary: 1689-1694, William: 1689-1702)

James II, Charles II's younger brother, was so unpopular that a group of politicians invited a Dutch prince, William of Orange, to invade and take over. William was married to James's daughter Mary. They reigned together as William III and Mary II.

Forgotten Sceptre

Mary II's Sceptre with the Dove was only used once, for her joint Coronation with her husband. In the eighteenth century, it was put away and forgotten. The sceptre was found 50 years later at the back of a shelf, covered in dust.

JAMES II 1685-1688 | WILLIAM AND MARY 1689-1702 | ANNE 1702-1714

THE HANOVERIANS
1714-1901

When the last Stuart monarch, Queen Anne, died without an heir, her cousin George, from Hanover in Germany, became George I. During the Hanoverian era, Jane Austen wrote *Pride and Prejudice*, Britain built up a huge empire, and the Industrial Revolution changed the country for ever.

George II (1727-1760)

King George II loved fighting wars, and was the last British monarch to lead his troops into battle. He fought with his family, too – as a prince, he argued so much with his father, George I, that he was banned from court, and when he became king, he banned his son from court, too.

Bonnie Prince Charlie

In 1745, Charles Stuart, known as "Bonnie Prince Charlie", tried to invade England from Scotland – he wanted to reclaim the throne that had been taken from his grandfather, James II, by William and Mary. Charlie was defeated by George II, so he escaped to the Isle of Skye in a boat, disguised as a lady's maid.

George III (1760-1820)

George III was the first Hanoverian king to speak English as his first language. He preferred life in the country to life at court, so he was nicknamed "Farmer George". He was also known as "Mad King George" – he suffered from mental health problems, and by 1810 he was too ill to rule. His son became Prince Regent and ruled in George's place.

George IV (1820-1830)

George IV didn't get on with his father, George III. He didn't get on with his own wife, Caroline, either, and he even locked her out of his Coronation. George spent lots of money on art and architecture, including the Royal Pavilion, an exotic-looking palace in Brighton.

George Frederick Handel

Handel was a German-born composer who spent most of his life in London. His best-loved pieces of music include *Messiah*, which is still performed around the world to celebrate Easter and Christmas, and *Music for the Royal Fireworks*, which was written for George II and performed at a festival to celebrate the end of a war.

1714 — 1837

| GEORGE I | GEORGE II | GEORGE III | GEORGE IV | WILLIAM IV |
| 1714-1727 | 1727-1760 | 1760-1820 | 1820-1830 | 1830-1837 |

Victoria (1837-1901)

Victoria became queen aged eighteen, after the death of her uncle, William IV. In 1840, she married her cousin, Prince Albert Saxe-Coburg-Gotha. They were very happy together and had nine children. Albert died in 1861, and Victoria was devastated. She wore black for the rest of her life.

The British Empire

During the nineteenth century, Britain was the most powerful country in the world, with an empire that stretched across the globe. In 1876, Victoria was made Empress of India, which she thought was the "jewel in the crown" of the Empire. She never went to India but she learned to speak Hindi and Urdu and she had an Indian advisor.

The Industrial Revolution

During the eighteenth and nineteenth centuries, new inventions changed life in Britain for ever. This was known as the Industrial Revolution. The first railways were built across the country, new machines made manufacturing easier, and people flocked to cities to work in factories. The telephone, the postage stamp and the bicycle were invented, too.

Kensington Palace

Victoria grew up at Kensington Palace with her mother, the Duchess of Kent. Originally, the palace was chosen as a country retreat by William III and Mary II, later becoming a popular home for royal families. Kensington Palace is the London home of the Duke and Duchess of Cambridge and their children.

Victoria and Albert's Children

Victoria earned the nickname the "Grandmother of Europe" because she arranged for her children to be married into other European royal families. Today, there are seven royal families in Europe, and Queen Elizabeth II is related to all of them.

1. Victoria married Frederick III of Germany
2. Albert Edward (Edward VII) married Princess Alexandra of Denmark
3. Alice married Louis IV, Grand Duke of Hesse
4. Alfred married Maria Alexandrovna, Grand Duchess of Russia
5. Helena married Prince Christian of Schleswig-Holstein
6. Louise married John Campbell, Duke of Argyll
7. Arthur married Princess Louise Margaret of Prussia
8. Leopold married Princess Helena of Waldeck and Pyrmont
9. Beatrice married Prince Henry of Battenberg

1901

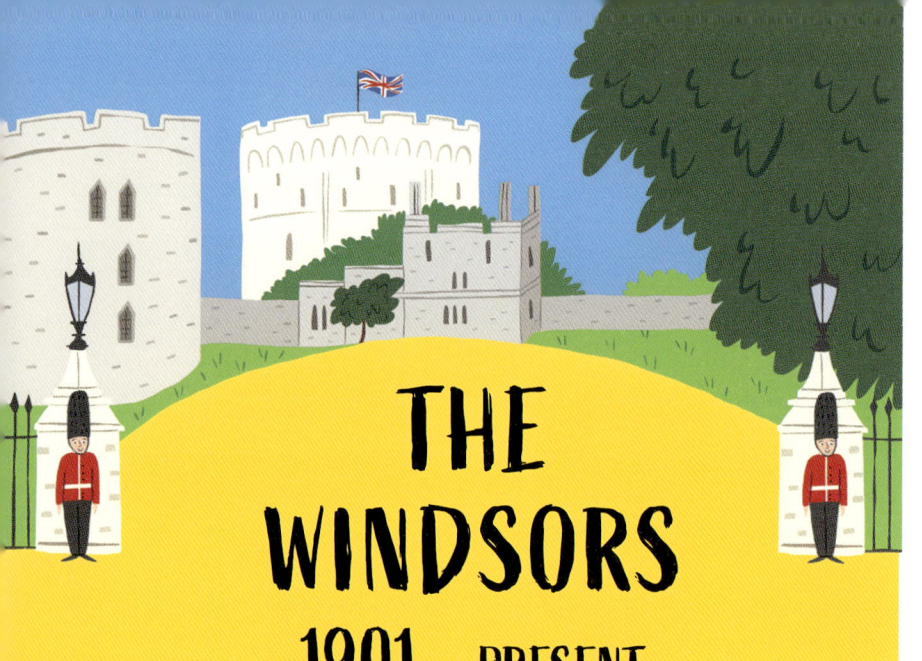

THE WINDSORS
1901 – PRESENT

When Queen Victoria married Prince Albert, the Royal Family took his name: Saxe-Coburg-Gotha. But when the First World War broke out, George V decided it sounded too German, so he changed the name of the Royal Family to Windsor, after Windsor Castle. The Windsors are still the British Royal Family today.

George V
(1910-1936)

As a prince, George V joined the navy. He loved sailing and even had a sailor tattoo on his arm, but he had to give up his career when his elder brother died and he inherited the throne.

The First World War

The First World War broke out four years after George V became king. The war was known as the Great War and "the war to end all wars" because it was so destructive. New inventions including machine guns, tanks and aircraft meant there were huge casualties on both sides. At first, people thought the war would be over by Christmas 1914, but it raged on until 1918.

1901

EDWARD VII
1901-1910

GEORGE V
1910-1936

The Christmas Broadcast

King George V was the first monarch to give a speech over the radio, on Christmas Day 1932. He decided to broadcast a message to his people every Christmas, a tradition that continues today.

Edward VIII (1936)

King Edward VIII wanted to marry Wallis Simpson, an American woman who had been divorced twice, but kings weren't allowed to marry divorcees. Edward had to choose between the crown and the woman he loved. He chose to marry Wallis, and became the only British monarch to voluntarily give up the throne. Wallis was considered beautiful, and Walt Disney is thought to have based his Snow White on her.

George VI (1936-1952)

George VI was shy and didn't want to be king. But when his brother gave up the throne, he had no choice. George worked hard at his new role, and became popular during the Second World War – he and his wife, Elizabeth, stayed in London even though the city was being bombed.

The Queen Mother

After George VI died, his wife became known as Queen Elizabeth, the Queen Mother, to avoid confusion with her daughter, Queen Elizabeth II. She died in 2002, aged 101.

EDWARD VIII
1936

GEORGE VI
1936-1952

1952

The Future of the Royal Family

The world has changed dramatically since the beginning of Queen Elizabeth II's long reign. During this time, the role of the monarchy has evolved, and media interest in the Royal Family has grown dramatically. Today, the Royal Family supports around 3,000 charities, carries out 2,000 official engagements and replies to over 100,000 letters a year!

Prince Charles

When the Queen celebrated her Platinum Jubilee, Charles became the oldest heir to the throne since William IV, who was crowned in 1830 aged 64 years, and the longest-serving Prince of Wales in British history. Charles married his first wife, Diana, Princess of Wales, in 1981 and they had two sons together, William and Harry. Sadly, Diana died in a tragic accident in 1997. In 2005, over 50 years after they first met, Charles married Camilla Parker Bowles, who became the Duchess of Cornwall. Charles supports a number of charities, particularly the Prince's Trust, which was set up to help vulnerable young people across the UK. Charles is also an advocate for a sustainable future and a proud environmental leader.

Royal Babies

When a royal baby is born, a typed notice is placed on a golden easel in the forecourt of Buckingham Palace to announce the news. In 2013, William and Kate, the Duke and Duchess of Cambridge, welcomed their first child, Prince George, and the news was tweeted for the first time in history, too!

Buckingham Palace

Buckingham Palace is the most famous of the royal residences. Other royal palaces include Windsor Castle, Kensington Palace, Sandringham and the Queen's favourite summer residence, Balmoral Castle. Buckingham Palace has its own post office, cinema, police station, clinic and offices, and is the place where many State events take place. On special occasions such as royal weddings, the Royal Family stands on the balcony of Buckingham Palace and waves to the crowds below.

Royal Weddings

A time of national celebration, royal weddings capture the heart of the country with many memorable moments. When Charles married Diana, the train of her wedding dress was over 7 metres long. On William and Kate's wedding day, Kate wore a tiara known as the "Halo Tiara", loaned to her by the Queen, who had been given it on her eighteenth birthday by her mother. For the wedding of Harry and Meghan, the Duke and Duchess of Sussex, 2,640 members of the public were invited to watch from the grounds of Windsor Castle.

The Line of Succession

The British royal line of succession is a unique and often complicated system that dates back to the seventeenth century. The Royal Family will live on through Queen Elizabeth II's children and her grandchildren.

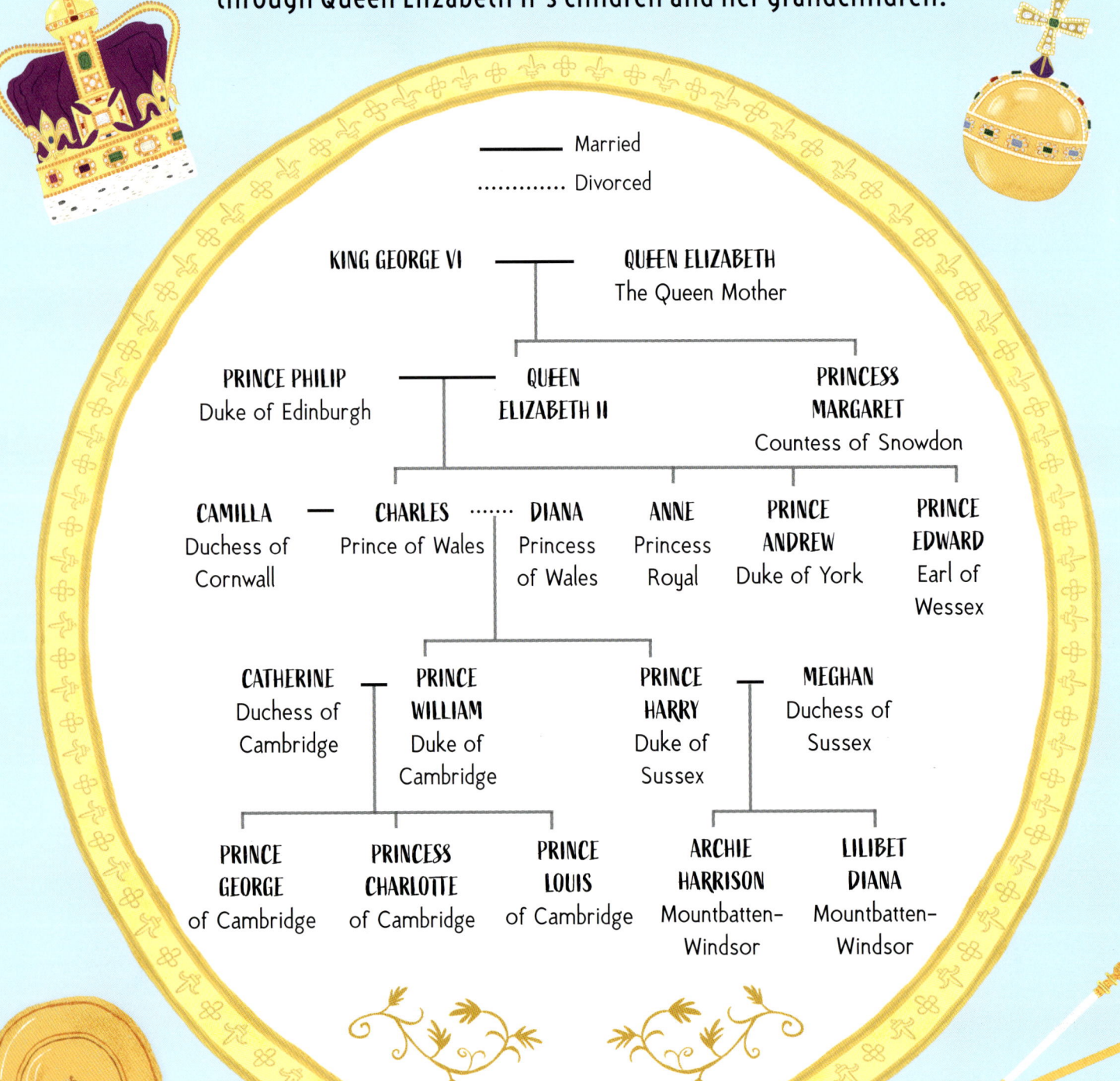

—— Married
·········· Divorced

- KING GEORGE VI — QUEEN ELIZABETH, The Queen Mother
  - PRINCE PHILIP, Duke of Edinburgh — QUEEN ELIZABETH II
    - CAMILLA, Duchess of Cornwall — CHARLES, Prince of Wales ······ DIANA, Princess of Wales
      - CATHERINE, Duchess of Cambridge — PRINCE WILLIAM, Duke of Cambridge
        - PRINCE GEORGE of Cambridge
        - PRINCESS CHARLOTTE of Cambridge
        - PRINCE LOUIS of Cambridge
      - PRINCE HARRY, Duke of Sussex — MEGHAN, Duchess of Sussex
        - ARCHIE HARRISON Mountbatten-Windsor
        - LILIBET DIANA Mountbatten-Windsor
    - ANNE, Princess Royal
    - PRINCE ANDREW, Duke of York
    - PRINCE EDWARD, Earl of Wessex
  - PRINCESS MARGARET, Countess of Snowdon